parallel equators

By the same author:

Pfft.. (2021)
how to spear sleep (2021)
the day the artists stood still—volume one (2013)
clouds in another's blood (2010)
Apples with Human Skin (2009)
what marian drew never told me about light (2007)
Sweeping the Light Back Into the Mirror (2006)

parallel equators

Nathan Shepherdson

RECENT
WORK
PRESS

parallel equators
Recent Work Press
Canberra, Australia

Copyright © Nathan Shepherdson, 2023

ISBN: 9780645651218 (paperback)

A catalogue record for this
book is available from the
National Library of Australia

Cover image: © 'Universal Mask of St. Stephen' (detail) by Gordon Shepherdson, 1990, photographed by Neil Griffith, 2022.
Cover design: Recent Work Press
Set by Recent Work Press

recentworkpress.com

for Gordon Shepherdson 1934-2019

Contents

u. your new design for the sun has one flaw.

our parallel equators only a handspan apart.

Assunta Strada

a.

we take our seats and wait for the cave to auction its echoes.

mixed memory on paper

Whiteley visits Morandi

when he died
i found me
living in my room
until now

until your head
falls into your lap
you will not see yourself
first hand

the second reality
in a third string field
attached to nothing
describes no one
to himself

a white heron
prepares to sip gravity
from a ceramic bottle
in Bologna

in complete privacy
a sample
however small

nothing is more alien
than art in the work of art
in itself

by avoiding the metaphysical
i grow fingernails
in the light

his glass womb
the perfect vessel
for silent opera

a life might only be
as long as the arm
you paint with
write with
or inject

there is no passage
to where you are
if you're there
telling yourself not
to breathe until
the disease captured
by sun in the window
is cured so theory
can forget why
it exists and comfortably
finish its speech
in the empty room
where saints continue
to polish the floorboards
by blinking

there are lessons
that burn the candle
the other way

this illusion at peace
with what it resents
allows skin to sleep
unattached to any form

three sisters in the shape
of a wife i will never have
thankfully take turns to rinse
my eyelids to leave them hang
on the back of a chair

all density sent to all corners
as i insert the fingertip
into subconscious surface

removing it
the energy returns
so i can remove myself

too relaxed
at the prospect of death
i realise i have never
found a head that suits
my appearance

on a palette the shape of a brain
dust legislates in tones
as organised as undecided time
kept deep in the glandular biology
of a simple brush

involuble pigments
set under the resonance
of a linseed cello

words cannot be trusted
in the company of art

tell a painting what it is
it will know you are lying

my method is to fill
canvas bags with memory
place them at the foot of the door
then calmly wait for the flood
i am told will never arrive

my purpose to defend colour from its ego

on an unsigned postcard of my work
sent to me by myself i read . . .

he had stopped working;
was going blind;
was readying himself for death;
had never visited Paris;

in sympathy i stretch out full length
on the table to observe the last pear

my nose an intimate companion
pressed to the hip of its ripening ballast

its solitary leaf
curled to its stem
in dry surrender

when they cut the tree down
the sap ran from the limbs
of my childhood

clouds that are still alive are still dead in here

to paint what i can see is to see what i cannot paint

a mirror is the ransom note anyone can read
but nobody chooses to pay

we kidnap ourselves by being alive

from the other side of the shark*

for B.R. Dionysius

cut with postmodern wit
i can carry the million pound tag
that will not release me
back into the wild

draw your outline on the glass
as you decipher the self
(in formaldehyde)
to witness again
how your mother pulled the teeth
you never knew she had
until you found them in your chest

the animal
you chose not
to cut in half
is the animal
known to leave
half an animal
in your hands

did we float
in this publicly listed company
along with the other shareholders
who invest in the potential
for our death

this animal ←
was born when a photograph
could only persuade us
in the negative

so step back into the water

lean forward in the polaroid

your trial bite is free
unusual for a killing
to be launched
immediately

a bite made
so gently the victim
is unaware

as a survivor
you came ashore to describe
how you were bumped
by something →

← taken aback
by the sight of blood
streaming from a dozen incisions
harp notes on the skin
demonstrating how a life
could have been
unbuttoned

so step out of the water

many attacks are nothing more

( ) than a →

catch/
hold & release/
exercise/

your childhood never knew
the colour in a polaroid
would not last

this is a notable exception to there

a moment we re/hearsed
that cannot take its big idea to the grave
until either the lungs or the laughter
subside

this line was thrown out
because it was not needed
because one nightmare is efficient enough
energy equal to the substantiation of itself
fuel in a vein
pumping liquid cinema
into a lonely tank
rivets scalded to pinched sleep
where images combust in a rib brazier
intent on self defence
against our own cold thought

drifting in our craft
you offer the assurance
that with fourteen lines
you can pull in sharks
by the metre

on the fourth day
the lines yielded a large *tyger*
which you towed ashore
and opened on the beach
belt-tight in an underglow of rutile glare
poorly shielded by wind-shook hessian

as you felt the bulging stomach
you went cold as i ran
as you ran your hands
ran my hands over a smooth dome
→ obviously
the head of the unfortunate

you have altered the head
by not noticing
it's there

you have altered the head
by not noticing
its face

this great blunt head
almost square edged
attacking a bait at speed
the teeth unmistakable
oblique blades deeply notched
rearward and cockscomb like
the flesh untethered from the bone
salted blue in a myth is deep fear
catapulted powerless to its red end

this great blunt head
almost square edged
abates its attack at speed
in its current life
unrolled over clean cartilage
is the physical prayer
is the swim in an uneven hunt
to bite off hands together in pairs
in communion in communion
incommunicado

your head was dismantled
by the fishbone
dreaming in your throat

every hour awash from every hour
the tide nothing but a broom
to sweep its infinite floor

items to recover
from the recovered animal
include

a lump of coal

a tattooed arm with rope around its wrist

a handbag containing a watch in perfect time

you have been sent here
to pay excise on lost memory

you are the only live bearer in this sentence

given the dubious honour
of evaluating every letter
to redecorate irrational probability
with the fresh stomach contents
from one suggestion

such an animal
is not easily brought
to the weighing station
much simpler to send it
to the auction house
to let an adman's account
swallow gold value added as fillings
to a theoretic smile

14

white belly to white belly
position switched you stand above
lie below your uncut gnathic beast
held palm to sweated palm
its skin again the handle to an art
taut *same-kawa* on a Japanese sword
as sharp as sharper than mutual emulation
the price too to not cut it in half
to see ourselves in the same body

on this same line
we are hooks set back to back
only to have our animal escape
by straightening one hook
and breaking off the other

our kiss can only consist of teeth

we circle in the moment before
our spiracles ventilate cold steam
unthought through necessary instinct

our eyes will be reported as being
'gleaming black' protected by objective spirits
living inside transparent white eyelids
which will slam shut across our vision
when we launch the attack
on each other

this is the only known instance
where two lives were lost
in one shark

the physical death
of impossibility
in the mind
of someone living

in water
the shadows are too skilled
to pay their ransom

the broken ocean
will push these broken eyes
to the unfixed surface
of our last eye
in space

i was not said to myself
because you named me
without saying anything

*Or: remembering when B.R. Dionysius & Damien Hirst (both wearing sharkskin suits) met in the bar of a luxury hotel—clinked glasses—but said nothing because they both knew Vic Hislop was still out fishing.

the poem drinks its own lips

for Glen Skien

4,4/3,7,4,2,5,2,5,6,6,4,3,4,5,3,5/7,4,5,4,5,10,
2,3,5,4,6,3,3,5,10,2,4,8,4/5,2,3,4,8,4,3,5,9/4,
4/2,3,3,4,2,4,1,5,2,9,2,7,4,9,10,2,1,5,2,4,4,6,
11,5,4,6,5,2,8,3,6,2,7,6,3,2,7,2,4,6,5,3,3,8,6,4
,4,4,4,7,3,5,5,2,4,5,4/4,5,2,4,3,7,2,2,5,4,2,7,5,
3,2,2,8,4,2,7,4,1/7/4,6,3,3,9,2,3,5,7,4,5,2,2,8,
4,4,3/7/2,4,4,4,5/3,3

next/time

our fingers will be bound
in black muslin
making sure
the pins avoid the nails

cuticle cups
grown over blank expression
in our flesh pink enough
not yet fully penetrated
by each separate moon

touch is the last disciple
from the first sensation

this/time

we can put them up
like a flock of blackbirds
in blister pack formation
unfollowed by a light
is each bird caught
cent/imetres a/part

from either perch
or breeding box
unable to provide
either egg or charity
as each object waits
for the oversize thumbs
that will push them
through the outer shell
of this inner wall

this image ←
is just one example
of an early form of
writing where tar
in an upturned head
is stirred with a

(feather)

true memory
has its birthdate
at its death
forgets what birth is
to remember what life
was

↕

nothing

in this room with wings

can fly

the eulogy of no from the funeral of yes

for Arryn Snowball

this is a speech
in silent bloods
without colour

in a panic of light
the cuff of a brushstroke
sustains the surface
to the surface (not there)
to embed its tissue sample
in nowhere (not there)
is nothing
but where we are
in one breath
lining this atmosphere
the pinhead becomes
the absent eye
thrown over its canvas cliff
that is (not there)
that is nothing
but where we are

(happily so) ←

with each breath
you are resigning the lease
for our tenancy in space

you stand in another vacuum
where the alarm is perpetual
in a world without ears

(here) is another echo

surgically removed
from one unsworn maybe
hand stretched
then left to soak
in umber brine

you learn to wipe out
another oversold dimension
with your skin

the simple method
to groom you with a species of doubt
called thought (   )

in the expanse of our judgment
is the judgement that wasn't called for
but is nonetheless heard

to paint
is to beg the silence
not to speak

to paint
retrieves the fact
from the problem
to cremate the thought
to inhale the smoke
from the fact

the grey whistle of a line
diving cold into the one clock
with no face

falling into an idea
with no hope of escape
is the escape

there are no sanctions
against the iridescent moments
in the soul

you have caught the train
with phosphorous wheels
hurtling the single track
in the spine

you have preserved the scent
wrung out of this turpentine economy

behind this picture
the dog is whimpering
for you to come home

but you are (here)
to look at a picture
in the same way
that rain describes itself
to water

there is no need
to look at a picture
in the same way
that rain describes itself
to water until tears
in their ducts
form glaciers

the painter must behave
as the ghost in the memory
of no one known

form fed
into the alla prima notions
of difficult birth

all is what it was
in a linen rucksack
left unattended on the sill
of the only window
to never close on its own
history

so forgive this theory
as it plots a terror attack
on the noun

lie quietly under the essay
where you stammer inertia
by leaving in
what you take out

pump heavy water
to the shape of a bridge
to drift across as always
to leave yourself
on the other side

mirrors are designed to sink
in their strange obedience
held lead–white
in the planetary axis
of the neck

without the frame
the picture cannot exist
within the frame
it is only a picture
until told it is a surface
only allowed to cast
first stones at its own sin
the blood never dries

because it refuses to be seen
until it can be distilled
into a handful of unsown words
about to decry their allergy to red

this is how ←
you undress granite eyelids
with the dusk

or spit trees
into a timber mill
in the dark

this is how ←
you check the lungs of an anchor
only half full of unheated plankton
hiding from the sleep & desire
in a whale tooth

or pull sparrows out of a storm
to check their leg-bands
for your name

this is proof in the story
of how a theory and an atom
were both awarded the same fight
in a split decision

passacaglia equations in chalk
play the wall note for note

this is how →
you mop the circle
to clean the square

the static
blocks the view
to reveal the picture

the steam
ushers lunglessly off their backs
in this livery stable for contemporary centaurs

only once in a life
is it possible to bury the ocean
in the body

you baptise the black hole
wrap it in a sheet
before passing it to your mother
to nurse it until you return to her
and show her the lead wallet
you picked up outside Einstein's house
and show her the notes made of gravity
counting them out on the table
and offering to settle the rent
well overdue on your memory

you match the pieces of yourself
to the pieces of the chair
/both already broken/
inside a double existence
where you are both required to sit down
to record the joinery in the other's form
until you both begin to spin
like spent filaments in a light bulb
once proud to have illuminated nought
inside shadows sold as acreage
inside a room the size of every question
small enough to conceal
behind the fingernail

of your choice

having removed the tape
the house feels like a barcode
for eternity

no more or no less
than what is reflected in the floor
as double agents depth & perception
are re-arrested at the border
of what is

give this language its script for confession
before you refuse to listen to what it says

welcome the dark angle that cannot be measured

black always enforces its curfews on form
and is best lubricated
with the skin from the lips

it takes the trouble to define
to hit the retina like a bullseye
dreaming its end in a hunter's pouch

a thousand dead mathematicians
will tell you there's safety in numbers
before they all sit up
and count to one

silent approach

your defoliant shadow leaves you with nothing but sunlight

crisp air swings its murdered hand
in contrast to the falconer's glove
that waits for your father to land

as the wasp stings the mirror your image swells

the tonal palette you emit from your displayed absence
yet to arrive as it takes your hand and you both walk
eyes closed through the crushed mineral state
into the monogamous colour theory of one man

the figure as a trenchcoat keyhole
imagines itself unmarried to an open door

in the nostrils of the approached and the approaching
sulphur unpacks the cold

in one downward stroke
the thermometer is painted over

at last count mercury was not elected
to the register of favoured poisons

simplicity is simply the simple white pill
on a push-mower tongue that is never swallowed

this is the possibility of who the coat carries in its pockets

lint as raw fibre unspun to memory
deep in the digestive tract of prospective touch

[... gust-powered ... the pincers
from a single chlorophyll claw
breaks open this mock ovoid head
to disperse the conscience in turpentine fog ...]

angles are never alone until they're measured

vertical + cranial = horizontal
vertical + cranial = horizon( )

grey poles as the three graces
sucked through the straw
of their own shadows

here is the restraint you sift through a soft valve
only to recapture it using an eyelash
as fishing line

the exotic servitude
with which you climb inside
plain things

the skin lisp
of the wall as it walks
through itself

the theosophical errand
you continue to run to yourself
in order to forget what the message is

as always or not at all
art allows us to comply with its request
to retrace the steps that never occurred

what you can't see is joined at the lip

what the eyes exhale to surface
though pores for thought
inculcated in sleep from medicated colour

your request to blindness
to confess its symmetry
will be ignored
will be accepted

they would have us sink worms
as supple tent pegs into each other's graves

the stained glass windows of the world are coming

for D Harding after Wall Composition in Reckitt's Blue 2017

never fall asleep in the rumour
that you're still alive

this is the anonymous knock
that again leaves a wheelbarrow
of candle wicks at your front door

this is the witness account of you
reaching through yourself as a dislocated being
to pull your body through yourself
to pull your body through
the handle of a shovel

this is a photo of you
ringbarking art history
to make the weird 360 smile
while brushing the critic's teeth
with an axe

this is the logic
of the whisper
that refuses to enter
the ear

when you sleep you glow blue

■

even as uncut diamonds
we're washed in this blue
as we suck on ourselves

our saliva sinks wells
into blue holes that do
not ask blue gravity to
collapse in inner blue
but instead propose a blue
place where it can sleep

even without ourselves
as an unus we are sent
to the other place where
we suck on other stones
either like us or as us we
are the blue river while
admitting in blue that the
blue time we have or unhave
as blue time is not time is no
time not time until it's spent
in blue as we count
not ever all or once
as our blue fingers fall
into the patient into the
patient blue mouth of
our unsealed memory

■

i have no hesi_tation
in describing that i am
my full self out there

i have no hesi_tation
as i relate and contradict
the contemporary world
through an immovable
sensi_bility

that act of copying
my full self produces
new interstices for
engagement with new
entry and exit points
from my full self along
a continuum in the act
of copying the continuum
of my full self as i point
out of the new entry and
point in to the new exit

from this original copy
of my full self a subsequent
copy can be made from an
original from an original
stencilled painting of a copy
of the original object from the
copy of the object stencilled
from my full self from this
original self of the original
object a subsequent self
can then be formed

when i sleep i glow blue

some of these forms
of my full self were even
unknown to us when we
visited them when we
visited them some of
these forms were even
unknown when we visited
these forms some of them
we visited were us

when forms sleep they glow blue

as sovereign bodies
as sovereign bodies
the haemoglobic equations
are squeezed from our veins
to nurture the algal bloom
in the single zero that has
all zeros in common with
my full self

now they say my full self
could drown in the single zero
but not before my full self
is given permission to peel
the skin from the anchor
not before i peel the skin
from my full self before my
full self i peel the skin from
the anchor before it drops

■

you offer
and in turn
are offered
the prayers
turned sour
by history

you offer
and in turn
are offered
the history
turned sour
by prayers

■

on the second day
of every fourth month
mouths open in the floor
to clamp the legs
of this silky oak table
in place

their stipple teeth leaving
pockmarks as splinter cavities
to hold burning rosary beads
inhaled into timbergrain
by their own smoke

your body is the single invention
of the chair you are sitting on
as your head stares back at you
uncooked & uneaten yet well salted
from the quarried perspective
of its granite plate

what you remember
is what you will forget to say
reduced to one word
in a scream that takes one hour
to pronounce

we coat our bodies
in the nutrient dark
of our language milked direct
from the knuckles of ancestors

from this day on
humans are forbidden

from appearing in the dreams
of animals

■

as you enter the space
your senses are shifted and turned
from how they were applied
in the corridor

the light drops away in space
the light drops away in space
the light drops away
heavily

the room and the walls recede
as your eyes adjust and you search
for content in the room content
in the room

throughout the investigation
the door remained silent
its double zed frame
flexed in bicep security
as the bolt lies as flaccid as
an unused tongue depressor

the key was hung on the other side
of what could not be escaped

in some ways in some ways
the kerosene silence is more powerful
than the scream

this is how

charcoal licks the body
with perfect lines

shadows reuse their ovalled blindness
to sink grammar into concrete meaning

shadows mistake themselves
for the light they came from

corners slapped into unconscious gradients
are tasked with repairing their own shadows
before sunrise

when the room sleeps it glows black

static must persist in movement to possess its sins

your role is to follow yourself home as your own perpetrator

loneliness can forge any signature without moving its hand

■

you are the inventor of blue static

kkqqeeeee…

when you can bury
my arms with a shovel
i'll stop digging

kkqqeeeee…

the reader says →

i am

but do not want to be
a tourist in this idea

kkqqeeeee...

the reader recounts questions
he did not ask the artist
in the interview they did not have

kkqqeeeee...

why do you choose to build thunderstorms by hand?

why is this keyhole big enough for your entire arm?

why can you forgive the light switch but not the light?

why does skin weigh more than water as the ballast in a ship?

if you separate the silicone from the weapon is the war still there?

does the overhanging body part on the plinth mean we're all going to fall?

when will the stained glass windows of the world arrive?

kkqqeeeee...

he measures himself /
into the architectural fillet
of amber glass / then lowers
himself / onto the lip / lowers
himself onto the lip /
of a whitened shelf / too small
for his largest concerns

kkqqeeeee...

undertheYvesweheareineKleinReckittsmusik
undertheYvesweheareineKleinReckittsmusik
undertheYvesweheareineKleinReckittsmusik

kkqqeeeee
kkqqeee
kkqqe

when you can bury
my arms with a shovel
i'll stop digging

kqe

■

this is the breaking up
and the dividing and the
signifying of land

i am interested in the piercing
penetrative force piercing pen
etrative force these stakes
make on the landscape stake
s on the land_
scape

these pegs are painted white
painted white and with that
white with that white pen
etrative force i am i am in
terested in what in what ha
ppens if they become black
ened if they become burne
d and reduced in that way
in that way i am interested i
n that process in that proce

ss of reducing and diminish
ing the stake's importance im
portance they hold quite often
quite often they're painted wh
ite so white will feature so wh
ite on the shaft of the stakes
and i think it will be quite con
venient quite telling a telling
binary between the black betw
een the black and the white th
e black and the white the whi
te superficial coating and the
erosion of that superficial co
ating the erosion and the ret
urning and the reducing to t
he black

burning it down then going
and burning it down then
going then burning it

removing it ←
taking that thorn
out of the side

physical boundaries
cartography boundaries
landscape boundaries
metaphysical boundaries
art boundaries

border lines
starts & finishes

when the stake sleeps it glows black

■

he threads the needle
with the light from
his grandmother's eyes
to thread the needle
with the light from
his mother's eyes
to find his own eyes
on the needle

this has the feel of hessian
but is actually skin contemplating
where the stiches must go

did hunger subside by looking
through the bright eyes of a potato
that once wore a crown to prove
the sack was empty but the threats
were not

and the draper who sells such things
is always in supply and always sold out

there is skill around the collar
sewn by fingers departed from
their evidence sewn with mohair
around the collar to give comfort
to necks braided with pain now
unchaffed by their absence

in memory your two mothers ripen
in your memory just as bodily
you ripen in theirs

■

when we eat ourselves in moonlight
the red lake in our brain
is no answer to a doctor's question
moonlight will trade everything
we know about it to bequeath us
our own insignificance

in mock celestial behaviour
the backs of our heads
pass between the other
to birth an uncircled eclipse
for our thoughts to feed on
for our thoughts to replace
every lost library card
with a tongue

when a tongue sleeps it glows blue

with a truth so enormous
so small it can't be seen
is not noticed until it's there
to consume what we are

embalmed in methylated resin
surfaces bid by removing the prefix
in impermanence to sing the fact
that botanical portraits will easily
outlive the flesh

you fall into the queue of bodies
waiting to collect their hands
from the cave wall to rejoin
themselves at the wrist within
their new departure

they banish the colonial graffiti WARD

under your reopened sky that has swallowed
itself complete while coughing sand
onto fossilised fingerprints
there before before existed

through the decline of the original
is the failure which ascends through
the mirror of the new

when a mirror sleeps it glows blue

■

one drop of blood from the sun
catches your shoulder blade

liquid pixels in airborne blue
wash through untimed distance
propelled by your shotgun mouth
over this post-neutral wall
your breath is caught

e.

you find yourself running a ponzi scheme for souls.

earth works

i.m. George Ilievski (1930-2018)

I

the man who can carry himself in his own pocket
can offer himself as a light
to death →

II

the overflow from a mountain submerged
in a cup of tea buries your organs
as fresh seed in breathing soil

III

a naked runner on a balkan beach
in full stride elasticised against the horizon
is passed by his finish line

IV

concrete lips on the wind press through reservoir ducts
like an architectural ocarina to make a music so low
only engineers hear it at night

V

swimming with the verbs in your new language
you marinate the vowels in a rich brandy
to warm the blood in your handshake

VI

both poet & physicist with line & equation as rope
scale the lorándite cliffs on your face
to activate neutrinos deep in your unmeasured eyes

VII

when the portrait sent its skin into unretinated light
to stare at what it couldn't see
to acknowledge & ignore the replica in itself ←

portable eyes remit subconscious colour in black

i.m. Alun Leach-Jones (1937-2017)

all gates fly open in the act of being closed

transcendent markers slice the spine like bread

there are no symptoms the illness cannot cure

again handcuffed with an ampersand

they send the stolen voice
of a crow to suffocate
the moonlight

this line
with no face
invents yours

they strip the gold from your veins
and melt it down
to the perfect ounce

it is rare for rain to remember where it falls

◙

the hull in your head
always lists to the starboard side
in this country without water
there are still ample chances
to drown the many selves
who claim to know you
& who claim to be you
& who form a choir

to sight-read the disintegration
in your name

to do nothing is to change

he built ships simply to deny them water

◉

it is christmas eve
and he/she/they/we/i/us
arrive to read the meter

finds it wrapped in bandages
soaked in azure wax

still

he/she/they/we/i/us
note the increasing
number of shadows
that graze behind
your eyes

he/she/they/we/i/us
suggest

to sleep so long
that your eyes
become opals

he/she/they/we/i/us
understand

the idea

to be certain of what you're seeing
but not certain of what you've seen

he/she/they/we/i/us
know

the tenant has settled
into his lease agreement
with death

and throw in an unsourced quote

'i am too tired to lick yourself off the mirror'

then he/she/they/we/i/us leave
muttering something about the relative merits
of keeping a full stop in your shoe
so that every departure can at least recognise
the colour of its own dismissive gravity
before the next step hits the ground

as close as the eye is as the eye
was to closing on everything
it remains open to who you were
to who you are as a flesh firefly
with unclotted wings in acrylic
deeply mined through the intestine
of your absent self

◉

here is the record of when
you sent the cartilage in your ears
to the foundry to be cast
as musical form

as a procedural homage
your accent was grated into a bowl
the words sifted out
the silence mixed in
with what is

using the over-ripe brains of philosophers for jam

using the under-ripe brains of poets for doorstops

old floorboards are used as tongue depressors
with nails intact

the room is alive
in me and i in it
as we respell another i
in the silence of each
wall amassed in the vertical
tides of brushstrokes scraped
from the fingerprint
of one clock

one clock
cone lock
one clock
cone lock
one lock
cone clock

to recalibrate this thing
once thought to be a soul
by fermenting yeast from the mouth
of a dead pronoun

◉

you simmer commas until they're ready to eat

in the end i felt it was pointless
just to move the comma(,) to the side
of the word and this side of the word
to the side of the word just to move
the comma(,) in the end

the between i am no longer
between no longer the between
i am

◉

observe this auto-cannibal memory
in its race with a lit wick

observe your enmeshed meditations
on gray via its american spelling

within the confines of circles
squared with the circle itself
comes a hidden square again

it was the beginning which finally
reached painting in the beginning
within context i see a stepping off
to a new theory to a particular point
you remember much of the painting
i was trying to eliminate i was trying
to get into the painting i think because
you lose the painting because i think

what is in the field is the field

what is in
the field is
the field

what's left is not what was there

what exists from
what did not exist
will not exist if it
exists

◉

there is a loose majesty
in the treason that turns
the halos of those without
imagination into wedding rings
for gods who are not believed

you grew skin over rocks
to throw through bone windows
when time wasn't looking

the gift to murder
a white surface with thoughts
immune from prosecution

the technique to tap
the veins in a blistered mirror
of its unanswered light

angles mouth-taped in numbers
that forgive the beautiful leprosy

of their illusion

◉

to lose touch
with the head
by touching it

even without one there is one

even without
one there is
one

your vision semi-dissolved
in small vats cupping equal parts
milk and rust

it's about now they replace
the rungs in the ladder
with your ribs

slow burn the rungs removed
until your memory decides to climb down
to use them as charcoal

here your fingers
are a liquid
to erode form

your eyelids once leaves
are death to green
in reverse

your hand as careful as rain

that will only breathe in
so it never falls

◉

i have named your shirts for you

dipped the first brush
into the corner of each eye
for your uncle

the method
to carry yourself to snow
without moving

where are the deluxe assignations
concocted in the imperial pharmacy
of all truths

◉

your welsh body a landscape irrigated with song

subcontracted entrails in light fed you to your discipline

your name disinterred by trespassing steam

for M

i.m. Madonna Staunton (1938-2019)

it was the ocean that sank
not the boat

& there is nothing miraculous
when the weather finds itself
devoid of air

the sun
reduced to ink
replaces all drawings
with silence

to listen for   /
but in no way hear   \

the spatula scrape
of gold dust and liniment being packed
into your four chambers

four score (+) the one idea
that you'll sleep in a different colour

which is not true
yet remains the truth

[stillife]

for Neil Griffith & Louise Williamson

EV2059

he soaks the light clean

trims the bark
that has replaced
his fingernails

adds more photons
to this shrinking pillow
for the dead

EV2043

this is proof
of our evaporative limp
into dust

even silence
loses its leaves

EV2064

we wait months
for the flower to grow
out of his mouth

watch it radar
its saliva-eased form
towards the sun
& die

>   <

his eyes open

EV2073

[still] in possession
of its fallen shoreline

an island
tipped to vertical
that only a thought
could reach

its colour
already drained via its stem
into your hand

light compost to shadow

EV2051

a vascular towel
to wipe bodies
off the wind

the pharmacy
of emptied seasons

EV2074

pleats in a gravity skirt
desiccate to chalk
that will never
write

light
ferments in space
ferments our eyes
inside this last sip of colour
before our bones rearrange
as words under the foot
of this uncut sod

EV2079

the last three flowers
as collapsed lungs of light

they were never picked
by hands we never had

water ridiculed from petals

the role of pollen
in the reproductive life
of the brain

EV2069

a coffin
for the tooth
of a rat

wondering
how a head
is made

he finds one
on his shoulders

EV2053

to stare at one thing
until a red apostrophe
plummets head first
into the black fur
in the body
of a photograph

in recline
our eye sockets become
a rain gauge

EV2044

three anterior clamps
to muzzle the respective noses
of Cerberus

the fragrance of departing light

these secateurs ←
are to cut off hands

EV2088

balanced surface fibrillation

butterfly mica diamond cut
through the cleared fog
of another passing season

the memory curve
saddled between knuckles
in a single stem

is this the day
we will note our initials
in the bark on the other's neck

EV2079

this is an example
of a thinking
attuned to plants
evacuated from green

this same outline
reference to its other outline
scolded by shadows
defended by light

from the flesh
of a chewed limb
thieved from former existence
comes a single-blink tongue
encrusted in electric salt

leaves sprout from the fingertips

your trunk already in the ground

orbit

i.m. David Shepherdson (1931-2019)

shadows tell our eyes where to sleep

risk averse to the living is the life
because even memory is chance
when you are whittled down to that alone
and left to inflate the heads of others
after you stop breathing

your wrist watch on a fence post
captures dust instead of time
as cattle walk past

out to sea
you somehow fish
without a boat

your body follows a small channel
in the giant fingerprint
on the water's surface

a satellite witness
who departs his orbit

the black hand of Badia Elmi

for Simone Gelli in memory of Billy Gelli (1965-2010)

i reverse history to put out the sun

spin the earth in its opposite direction

nurse words like tired babies
until they explode

you are in the hunt
for the animals in your room
in the morning you find them
grazing on your chest

don't worry if the teeth are not yours

white is their permission
to lower these anonymous jaws
over your head

i turn my head
—thumbs into crown—
inside out
—fingers under chin—
a rubberised retreat
of the biological object
making no difference
to its appearance
either way

what is one to the other
is the other to the one
what is one to the other
is the other to the one
salt & pepper skulls
slide outward to bobble
on shoulders left & right
before glancing at each other
to slide inward and kiss
like two Eastern Bloc leaders
in a newsreel

at this time of year
my breath is held for a week
to allow me to interpret silence
as i organise the Carnival of Empty Streets
so i can draw the route for truant shadows
while they hold their parade
for the benefit of closed doors

the loose skin of your brother
follows behind

his husky voice
in duet with a scrape of leaves
wind dancing on stone
as the grey choir
feeds his tongue
into the ground

one day we will notice his face

on a hand-coloured chart
used to identify edible fungi
and when the barometer puffs its cheeks
and rain is ladled in correct portions
temperature will copulate with tremored light
as his scalp emerges in the undergrowth
earth smell in a spore's thought
waiting for the stem to feel its cut
from memory

these shapes
that we pull from our mouths
that we fail to recognise
are words

even a chestnut
recognises an ember
in its own shape
polished brown to pupil black
a small brain unshelled
cooking in promises of saliva

too poor to put our heads in the fire
we become rich by mining the smoke with a sigh
undressing the arrows before they go through the heart
offering ourselves the deeds to untitled happiness
a fool's language in a bird's voice
we count life into its alphabet of coughs
the rooster's claw on the hen's throat
although she has already won
his attention

it is said that her son
exhaled helium into the abbey
so as to lift it from the hill
while gravity occasioned sleep
the pilgrims floated inside
and wore the lunette arches
as sandstone helmets to dissolve their sin
which flowed like greyest blood
from their baffled eyes and ears
yet had the smell of burning pine

this is our lady of the helmets

the structure of her lips
tells me her hands are made of ice
snow always falling from her palms
unless she clamps them together in prayer
she is winter in summer
ankle deep in a slurry of zeros
from all parts of his kingdom
the story says that she once threw
her breasts into the river
which froze before the traveller's eyes
yet her breasts grew back
into their place over one night
so she could bless her milk
into the sudden hunger of every infant mouth
without the milk becoming rancid

this is our lady of the snow

her sister is the same person as her sister
her person is the same sister as her person

her sister is the same person as her sister
her person is the same sister as her

a fresh clementine
unpeeled in her mouth
in order to discover
the tree is still attached

in the crypt
three perfect squares
on which to play hopscotch
with god

the photo
from the top step of the house
plants three mulberry trees
and two parallel shadows leaning
towards our existence steadfast
inside their one note waltz
believed into a different winter
that always pronounces dead
but can never kill
the triangle

and to pretend more words
under the name of my brother
you might say to these mulberry trees
be ye plucked up by the root
and be ye planted in the sea
and they should obey you

they are strange timber joints

whose arthritic wrists can still bend the sky
thickset forearms of botanical certitude
that push through to weigh down their Tuscan crust
their new pruning gives up sap soaked canes
to weave in situ wicker chairs for deceased family
because the triangle is quick to remind its fact
that you are the last corner of your own square
season on season the fruit arrives
a tricolour vexillum graded with sunlight
where each full term pregnancy blister-ripe in temptation
is requited on the tongue

reduced to a diagram
trees 1 & 3 offer us vaginal trunks
and as old men in 2034
we will be invited to climb inside
to congeal with and to be renewed by
the menses flowing after the millennial ovulation

this is where Pyramus in love
sank so deep into celadon clay
his body calcified by the seeping Elsa
in such momentous circumstance alone
where all the water runs backwards
worms of an uncultivated kind
turned his silk garments to original matter
his brain wrapped in the spattered laundry of a lioness
mistakenly mashed in torment
was used as cold plaster
to smear the crack in the wall
that began his death

talking of words

for which i have no speech
fingers through the hair of intonation
tongues fall instead of vine leaves
onto autumn ground

the false alarm in history is to know it exists

rabbits dream their scale model of time in a warren

we are the same face eroded by the stone collar of our arms

our skulls crafted into jugs
with two spouts from the sockets
to pour new wine

our eyelashes carefully picked
are added to the pot
as black saffron

our eyeballs line up
under the forgiven oak of an olive press
still produce oil despite the lapse in centuries

on this day
it will be the onion
that cuts your newborn eye in half
in order to cry

the dot on its i
is the tear that separates
its twin letter set
in the mirror of its spelling

i did not change my mind
and next day went to the wood
to be killed

i killed a man and killed him
to kill him once more
i killed a man and killed him
to kill him once

not as dead as death i am
not as dead as death i am not dead

in one pocket
the marble finger of the famous author
as entire and sound as it ever was

in the second pocket
a lump of charcoal known for the miracle
that it will always regenerate its original weight
even if worn down to fingernail levels in its use

the black hand
remembers being drawn
on the wall
behind your head
above the stairs
that go nowhere

its long fingers
an indigenous graze
marking its descent
to a rendered edge
precisely one second
before it let—→ go

the left thumb
purported to be
our evolutionary difference
was easily defeated
by a flat surface
was virtually removed
by regressed illiteration

a mask crawls from grime gesso
a watermark trapped in a brick shroud
its chin rubbed mute by unclaimed luck
it smells us to where we are
cracking its cheek
with an awkward stone stitch over its right eye
an in-scale scar traced over Via Francigena

there are no handles in heaven

we cannot be removed
until we are here

behind this bolted door
followed by one drop of sweat
draining into each other's pores

as we walk the black line
in our approach to its mustard proportion
the lone sentinel pine raises its colossal eyebrow
to implant us into our own sight

you point out the two bells
where your parents have lived
since their passing

the bells never ring
because their bones are too soft
made soft by the lineaments rubbed deep
by your memoried action

the bells ring

i.

when a lefthanded dog woke to find its feet.

the water carries me to myself

for Luke Beesley

I.

i dam the river with my hand

cake enough words
between my fingers
to stop the water getting through

the bodies start to pool

eddy to touch up
against each other
some in small whirlpools
like seeds wanting to germinate
into a headline wanting
to send their first roots
through a statistician's hand
unable to record
what he won't see

i spray-paint numbers on their backs

II.

his spine turns to water

the ribs common tributaries
relaxed into a new map

granular bone
just sediment
in the memory

again

the cartographer is served
a cormorant's eye on toast
for breakfast

III.

only on a king tide
could the water climb
to the historical mark
in her throat allowing
her tongue to float
onto the next word
in a sentence at least
800 years old

water might find its own level
but it can't find its own words

he said he could not write
about anything
he had never seen

IV.

i drink your skin
until only water
is left

to finalise your limbs
i wash my face
in your chest
deoxidise brackish blood
to set its clearest metaphor
without feeling

if you noticed the word
shallow in this sentence
you were mistaken

V.

my father sets his head
on fire and throws it
into the river

resurfaces it with a bullock's face

his horns full of all
his possessions with nothing
left inside

saved from the fall by the fall

this is an approximation
of the pattern of ripples
he creates when he blinks

he has never remembered his name

VI.

did you fall in the water
or into this abstraction

curled by the eel
in a submerged bell
a brass suction cup
hiding unalloyed sound
like an unpatrolled love bite
on this estuarine neck

one follows all nowhere

the flow only one way
to here ←

sleep is half the miracle
that never happens

soon the mouth of the river
will return to use you
as its straw

VII.

no longer asleep

i am still
walking over my own shoulders
on a bridge made of myself
my arms commanding
both sides of the river
to handles

safely across
i signal for the others
to proceed

my shoulders
a populated yoke
under the weight
of thousands i stand up
tearing a new cliff
into each river bank
my sudden legs
atlantis-like pylons
grown into oyster pants

bereft of an idea
i invoke the motif
of gigantism

i tried to invent
a different scenario
but this is all
i could think of

to mend the narrative
i must write something
such as

now it's their bodies
that fall like rain
into the swollen torrent

it's just another shape
that fools the senses
into art

you may be losing interest
but don't forget i made it
to the other side

perhaps you were
looking at one thing
while i did something
else

escape
in order to drown
drown in order to
escape

he just wanted to wash
the meaning from these words
at the river's edge

hold the thing
to the light
that wasn't there

i will put a chair
on the surface of the water

and read everything
but the bible

poems before i knew you now i know you

for Elisa Biagini

uno

(39+61-56-36-6-1=1(

i sent you one tooth a day
to make the longest month
without a name

because of this ←

but in spite of that →

we no longer floss
between the other's
thoughts

in 2 days

an elderly couple
walking a pair
of black whippets
will find us
stripped & sleeping
in the dentist's chair

outside (   )
our house

due

(39-61+37-19+6=2(

playing tennis
with the equator
as the net

the rally
increases speed
as we move closer

(→   ←)

a cartoon volley
of full stops
in one point
until i slice
my backhand
to drip your blood
on the centreline

tre

(39-61+45-6-13-1=3(

we iron our faces

steam coming
from our tear ducts

we crease in
immaculate lines

from painless mask
to perfect square

put them
in each other's
pockets

in case
we need them
for later

in case
we need them
now

our mirrors hang
for treason

quattro

(39+61–38–36–16–6=4(

my tongue as biltong

you break off a bit

comment
that it's spicier
than you expected

wonder
if different languages
would affect the flavour

the time before this ←

my tongue
ended your mouth
dripped to its different
reason

cinque

(39–61+21+6=5(

you ask me
why i don't use commas
in my work

i like to keep them
between my toes

until winter

sei

(39+61–54–63+16+9–3+1=6(

just because
every hair
is a/
wick

doesn't mean
you should
set them
a/light

&   &

we challenge
the next page
to leave our
spine

we had our organs made
into an unfreighted table
so we could not take
our place at either
end

an upturned house
provides a convenient way
to measure what is
empty

sette

(39+61-20-96+31-9+1=7(

for alternate hours
we place the snail
on our foreheads

allow its unconjuncted vision
to explore undergrowth
in our eyebrows

otto

(39+61–50–69+3+16+9–1=8(

you stand at the sink

fill a glass with water

with my left hand
i sweep up your hair
from the nape of your
neck

i put my right hand
inside the marsupial pouch
at the back of your
head

to check that new words
are attached to lactating
thoughts

nove

(39+61+16-96-13+9-13+6=9(

when you are told
the world can spin
on one syllable

this poem
will be
complete

dieci

(39–61+19+13=10(

having removed
the bones from a
loaf of bread

you realise the knife
is my hand

(not our father's)

undici

(39–61–13+31+6+9=11(

the sugar
nowhere to be
found

following the death
of your favourite
teaspoon

dodici

)61+39-15-69-3-1=12)

silent shoes
made with skin
from the ears

even the truth
can't hear us
walk

tredici

)61–39+16–36+19–6–3+1=13)

with a wad
of fresh memory
& some creme cleanser

our skulls end
polished to the status
of a mirrorball

quattordici

)61+39+21-91-16=14)

& again
our ears
are deemed
as not be-
longing to th
-is species

each word/an
accusation/to
fondly/remember
/its crime

quindici

)61–39–14+13–6=15)

this water pooled
in this saucer

is more than
enough

to drown any
relationship

sedici

)61+39+27-63-91+36-1+9-1=16)

to prove i am not
lying

i press my eyes
in/side a book

stand on it until
my big toes blink
and gradually recognise
who i am

diciassette

)61+39-21-93+31=17)

as/expected

you defer
to your
shadow/to
answer/the
question

\

lean back
in the chair
you are not
sitting on

diciotto

)61-39-32+36-9+1=18)

with skill &
gentle strength

you pull out
my spine
with a corkscrew

(/winecork sound
through the crown
of my head   )/

a xylophone
for comedy

a clothesline
for shirts with
3 sleeves

diciannove

)61–39–34+63–36+1+3=19)

or the day
we spent listening
to stones through a
stethoscope

until we heard
                        one
goad its own
                        gravity
into an
unworded

                        vein

as special
mascara

are we

the scent of the
immaculate con
-clusion

venti

)61+39-31-91+31+19-9+1=20)

i hang your skin
over the chair

let white plates
sing their clean
chorus to bait
unfilled mouths

you hang
my skin
over / over
the chair

absence ensures
we are

      (here←)

ventuno

)61-39+16-16-1=21)

you open
the oven
door

birds fly out →

you open
the oven
door

i fly in   ←

ventidue

)61–39+0–0=22)

you cut your
self in half
with a
leaf

empty every
step from your
legs

rub your mother's
tears into your
feet

3 small engines

for Maria Zajkowski

3 ←   our deaths
                are not reported
                to ourselves

2 ←   we report
                our deaths
                to each other

1 →   no report
                is ever worth
                its reading

O.

she notes the patch of vulcanised rubber on my lung.

rain as narrative

for B.L.

Edda Dell'Orso feels clouds form on the roof of her mouth

cumulus pinatas struck with sluice gate sound
her tongue an Italian canoe adrift in wordlessness
(i capsize) to be sucked through a waterfall between her teeth
my head a murmuring piano hammer in saturated felt
bound to its unconscious chord inside a mossy rock
the release point for blood into the rapids
to livestream its current list from every forgetting
the warm red is turned inside out to cold blue

the weather prediction is for more sleep

lungs the size & shape
of sugar cubes dissolve
in monsoon thirst

it's easier to drown words than rats
and easier to talk to rats than people
as their feet sink into the mirror
and their tails tourniquet our ears
(so much so) (so much so)
that we did not hear the story
about the one apostle who had a lisp
and for sport the others would confect ways
to trick him into saying 'soul'

(so much so)

we did not hear their laughter being separated out
and pinned through its thorax

for charismatic posterity

(so much so)

i donated one finger
on each of the seven days
of creation

with only the thumbs
and a right index finger left
the proposal is made
that i can win the others back
if i can find a broom
small enough to sweep
the atomic weight from all objects
towards a front door opening slowly
at the last known address
for conceptual touch

in our private apocalypse
angels drain the lees
via a bung beneath the eyeball

we were tasked
with removing the skin
from the face of the waters

this was our last chance
to flood the memory
to save ourselves

cue three flute notes
dreaming three notes from a flute
by the riverbank

inside a refracted raindrop with John Ashbery

we clock the curve in our Popeye forearms
as John throws out the anchor from the tattoo
as an attempt to impede our fate-sped flow
as handblown bodies slipped in gelatinous glass

we hit the ground

the naked driver

for David Malouf

uncover the hand in the dust
to become the dust
the hand is

in memory is the auction unceasing
where a flat voice bids with silence
until a gavel pops the bone balloon

& imagination repercussed into phosphorous
strikes each face in the only mirror there is
because one light succumbs

to speech carrying ears as change
in its pockets a pair of cloth mouths
pressing space to its view
of the birth of birth
in a comma

you woke the river to the flood on your lips

chamber music bowing pylons under a bridge to self

the body worn to sleep before dinner is eaten whole

the body packed like a spinnaker awaits open ocean

canvas nerves frayed to the horizon
donate their giant eyelashes to:

(cartography)

this is why ←
the left margin of this poem

is Boundary St

this is how ←
your head is maintained
as a block of flats
with all occupants assembled
at your door

(either)

1. → you have never been here

(or)

2. → you never left

dissolve two heads in a glass of water
in order to drink the next thought

contradiction plants the flower
in the shadow of the flower
until it blooms in your head
& one cut flower
is not placed in your thoughts
but is placed in the vase
on your mother's grave

your chest again persuaded to dirt
as your nipples are watered
so two new flowers undoubtedly grow
not with the scent of a flower
but with the smell of a shadow
invested in the capillaries of each petal
is each thought also cut
& placed in the vase on your chest
without water

not to make the thing remembered
is to make the thing to forget

once a year the lid is removed
from the characters you create
heads in a barrel still confident
their teeth are white

you impersonate language to act as yourself
dance surfaces to counterpoint in a well read eye

now you wait for the naked driver
to buckle in your subconscious
to pick you up to signal left or right
to build the small orange suns
that herd your decisions into another sentence

without reason art continues
to frame the core samples
it has no permission to take
blood left on the page will drain away through the next full stop   .

colour pools to gladly affect the sinus inside biomosaic vision

this tender conceptual blue
you use to baste my eyes
wringing out the sky
one drop at a time
until sight is returned

frozen hands

for Felicity Plunkett

frozen hands shatter before they touch

words pulled at either end (end)
become black lines bundled
in a square inch of skin
surveyed and cut from the fore
head

when they attach leeches
to your memory you know
the predicted digestion
via common sense
is not far
away

you also know you
must consume the liver
in your conscience as
nourishment to maintain
the unlikely necessity
of yourself as a personal
god

now satiated
and drowsy
you see
black mermaids
face down
in water

withawishboneshape
deucalyptyoutweeze
rthemontoyourton
guetoreincarnatet
heirtailsincisedto
newlipstonewmo
uthsadozenfolda
syourheadinflate
sadozenfoldinsid
eitsnewlanguagea
sdeadasitbeganou
tsidebutnotexclus
ivetothelastwillan
dscanttestamento
fporcelainhopesun
glazedandbreakingi
ntounlistenedvowels

now we are
not the same
as we are
now

a naked inevitable
totally at odds
completely the same
as a well-dressed fate

because is adept
at shaving the head
that is always absent
because it is always looking
for (where) it buried
its bone

(1 a 1). your ears were passed in at auction

(2 b 2). you heart heritage listed as a trinket

(3 c 3). your fingernails thankfully replaced by mirrors

clouds weigh the truth
before we see it
rain in our skulls

the thread you cannot see
in this page is blue (where)
most would say 'like a vein'
but that's such an obvious
correlation and (this) requires
more imagination than (that)
but i guess we won't know
until we cut it will we (will we)

one umbilical breath
satisfies the twin impulse
of separate lungs in different bodies

moments after death
the chiropractor and calligrapher
shake hands before ripping out our spines
elegantly ply both into an ampersand
convert it to a neon sign
installed in the front window
of our family home / to be
switched off / on the day we were
born / to be switched on / off its own
back / which had our backs /
on the same day we will die

the liquid we drink from the hair
line fracture in our comma
keeps us alive

so leave the best percentage
of your body inverted in the ground
exposing your crepe myrtle calves
polished to bark-hard knots
with missing toes pruned each year
as a standing invitation to spring

are we now
not the same
as we are
now

two diamonds
wholly unlaced
with their own light

as compressed beings
we sleepwalk the memory
in this land until it opens
its jaws

your orb-empty hand
pushed through the (i&f) rigours
of engineering its hallucination
is shown to possess enough strength
to grasp a shrunken moon

without doubt
thinking would be unable
to water its excuses

there is no point
visiting yourself in prison
when you're already there

but you're glad you do

coated

for Kathryn Roberts

what we determine
are we not yet determined
to say

convinced of an autumn
when faces will fall
instead of leaves

time redesigned by fools
is always lost always in the end grain
of a lip cut through

even without breath
the snow still falls
in our lungs

a chair on the roof
waits for its window
to land

no movement
is not the same
as not moving

... learning to cry without eyes

after Michael Parekōwhai's The World Turns

this is where Hannibal's keychain
fell to earth

where abstraction
bent the key
to itself to lock
itself in & out
at the same time
we will meet at
the same place we
never go because
we can't find the
right feet to fit
the wrong shoes

this is where we stand
to watch a chair sit on itself

the grass square between its legs
inside a moat of absent feet

hollow dirt lisped to dust
followed trouser-length into a yawning river

weight unable to distribute itself
weighs nothing

two bronze eyes
confess to being cannon balls
reincarnated centimetres
above the titled ground
they never hit

this thought abseils a backbone

this forehead inverts a continent

did Peter Piper pick a pack
of pachyderm puns?

how many packs of pachyderm puns
did Peter Piper pick?

in the equation of knowing
what not to know
a marsupial topples gravity
with a scratch of its ear
recording every detail
in fleetwood prose

(the word not written here
was of no use because it was
not capable of describing
an animal there is no use
for the animal because
the word for animal is not
animal enough)

this is where
our dark haired Eve
had her hair cut
by something much sharper
than the well-funded wit
concealed in a 5 tonne sculpture

this is where
our dark haired Eve
fed her apple to the kuril
as she unthreaded mangrove seeds

off its battered tail
to put them in her mouth
one (by) one

she won't speak to you in French
until she's dead

twofold

for Eve Fraser

time equals its distillation in colour

a twofold remark
from a senate of atoms
that have never ceased
to travel

arrival & departure
for ephemeral language inside
the liquid lens that transforms
the bay into a telescope
pointed at space

the arms of the island
pull flesh satellites
from our eyes

a school of disembodied hands
flirt cursive script onto the underside
of their saltwater scrolls

shadows crimped
by the telepathy
in our smallest fingers
still afloat in the unclosed
mouth ready to swallow
dying light

the sky cremates
what's left of the day
in gaslit blue

~

these words are simply
an awkward measurement
of what they describe

this will be the method
used to vaporise your skin
within the lungs of this landscape

the bloom green
in thoughts gathered to observe
their own defoliation

as we invisibly ladle ourselves
into the irregular mirror
untethered from our abstraction

shorebound as a breath

the skin is sent to name the body

for Massimiliano Mandorlo

pain is hired to oversee the glass breeding program in mine eyes

i am the elastic substance they bind around the sun i am

one ember on one tongue expands to the mouth an amphitheatre

their ears without compassion
can have sex with this sound
and walk the forty-five miles
to where my nerves end
to continue to correct the grammar
of debased physical form
by doubling my limb length
just inside & just outside
this unrepentant crevice
full & unfilling with blood
devoted to keeping my shadows
(alive)

their knife is my father's hand

its tip orienteers the line to cut lip from gum
vowel mussel shucked from its mouth
to let the teeth protrude like Ionic pillars
doused in holographic haemoglobin

the radiant gristle
of ears departed
from their skull

eyelids turned inside out
finally hold the light
from the other side

hair bagged by its scalp
becomes a nest for unseen eggs
rich in predictive faith

the underwhorl of my crown
the last forgiving entrance
from which one self leaves in two ways

the complete self made incomplete
made into the complete garment
to fit all other men

my gospels were never found

though i hid them under my fingernails
expecting them to burst like spores
when they ungloved my hands from touch
saddling lifelines with amended measurement

my legacy a few words on desiccated papyrus
transcribed through a cough of Armenian dust
to pronounce one attributed guess

.. .. .under .his.. .
thought.. ... . our
.. .hands dissolve . . . .
.... .blinding .. himself.
.. . . to our ... . needs .. ..
. our.. . .. father . .. . .. .crushed . .
.. weeping ... . stars . .. . with ..
.... his .. eyes . ..

sometimes violence is so pure
it is the sin that saves us

walls carry the inconsolable weight of our thoughts
and we walk through them without blinking
because the acid in our tears burns through each other's masks

after the body was taken down
my heart was thrown against the wall
to splatter into the maker's face

and his spirit pulled on my lungs as slippers to traverse the land
still breathing i push mortgaged air through the veins in his legs

and from my original body
i donated the 12 thoracic vertebrae
one to each apostle

my 24 ribs their 24 arms
that float to embrace my silence
like boats moored at the sternum
by a whisper as the reddest of sunsets
dissects the cage with one harmonious line
across my static mass of raw flesh
that resembles a bay teeming with miracles

and when my sinew is nothing but ether
my bones will wash up on their own shore
and they will be so heavy
that only children can lift them

now depicted and painless
preaching from a metamorphic book
bone has further ossified into marble
my body draped with my famous skin

as my left toes ascertain the edge of everything
as the plinth locks my surface to one idea in buried space
while Marco d'Agrate hammers his sentence into a joke

the sound only slightly louder than Praxiteles' laughter
set in aesthetic time before the saviour was born

as someone
who was not known
to himself
i am now known
to others
for my unknown
(words)

in this moment i am saved ←

death loose in my pores engineers a floodplain in my maker's eyes

i am followed →
but leave dual shadows
behind

i am found so many times i am lost as i am eaten

head down
my polluted body
stuck to the inner trunk
of this crucifix

i look upon my unpolluted skin
hanging like dripped paint
head up
on smooth bark flayed
from the same cross

the skin is sent to name the body Bartholomew

the body is sent to name the skin Nathanael

dual shadows as seeds from the same light burrow in this earth i am

eleven hours

for David Stavanger—Berlin birthday

this time your shadow is clay

as you take yourself for a walk
without a lead the city's skin
on projection reels you animate
a treadmill of images where memory
is unpicked but ripening in black
& white you end up cast as Hermes
in a peak cap on sampled ground

this is the place
where consonants
are stacked in crates
and stored wholemindedly
at the back of the throat

it says on the label
this bottle of saliva
has been pasteurised
to make it safe
for consumption

can you think
of another way
to say can you
think of another
way not to say
anything

where is where it is

is is where it was

was is where you were

i put this full stop in a box → ◘
and ask that you bury it
under a linden tree
to instill my presence
in a place i've never been

memorials are just as useful to fiction

now that you're there
i want you to stick your tongue
on the envelope instead of a
stamp

post? mark?

you have bought the right
to study the entomology
in an umlaut

in eleven hours you will be someone else

the notebooks of Mr & Mrs Emeritus

ironing the crease into her lung with your breath
the six words in end steam over blue charcoal in her eye

your hands arrive in separate envelopes on different days
and they are addressed to each other

even the earth in its eyedropper is not medicine to our mouths
it's the milk dispensed through holes in a flute that keeps us alive

Mr & Mrs Emeritus explain on the hour that death is a democracy
and that our last vote counts towards nothing

this tear in her quilted lip is also a landscape
a sharp pencil probe into gloss flesh to rescue unconscious words

nowhere remains the last kiss before birth
a plagiarised soul copied in perpetuity until it (is) the original

this is where we stand to watch fate giving birth to doors
in an unpopulated administration always open because it is always closed

at night the surveyor marks new graves with luminous spit
in day the ground shrugs its smile from a sleep-platoon of obedient rectangles

walls quiver in this orbiting box that holds a planet
bends in to bend out under pressure from every animal breath

reduced to two people we are each one half of the world
the equator the solitary vein that ties us at our waist

(or) we could take the black bars from an equals sign
and each break the other's neck to demonstrate true love

it's easy to swap the flour for the dust when making blood cake
the bits we eat of each other make us whole

i am never asked because i am not the answer
but bees land in your ears to enter the hive

submerged in a bath tub full of honey we applaud our impossible action
what can't be heard and what can't be imagined (is) what's in front of us

this is our chance to perform an encore to two empty chairs
eight legs without fangs still immobilised by venom from separation

we crack light bulbs under our armpits by the dozen
to make sure we can't see where we are

we set three owls on fire every eight hours
so we can see where we're going

these deep pockets we had tailored into our thighs
will allow us to hang on to our femurs when we crash

in an emergency the glass in your fingernails will break
touch the first alarm from which we evacuate the skin

and memory thrown into still water can supress its sound
overhaul emanation to reverse ripples in from the outer edge

this page is a ghost expecting to be haunted by its signature
black marks that repeat the surface into a white choir of denial

form is a lonely banker too wealthy to be seen
standing on your shoulders lining up the coin with the slot to not let it go

unbelieved as feathers to a head suddenly account their embezzled sky
drawn back & forth the horizon saws our self-conception in two

side-by-side-head-to-toe-holding-hands covered in fresh colostrum
we lie in a giant wound and wait for an absence to feed on (or) reject one body

red~prayered

for Sandra Selig

/in suspending yourself
as a red line
to such an extent
that you are no longer

visible

because you are there/

/i send myself
to the corner
to face the wall/

/i imagine my veins
in the same configuration
of what (you) see/

/i imagine the smoke
coming from your eyelashes
as you sleep/

/having tapped the head
of each nail with this question

could describe the hammer/

how sleep designs a mirror

walking through stone
and into measurement
i cut my colour
from the sun

tuning another hand
to the same splinter
is how ambition
attracts the company
of rust ←

what is this order of bones
restacked in a pyramid
every 24 hours
in lipless ritual
on a bed
that dreams of sleep
is why i'm here
patting the stoic dog
that has been trained
to carry my skull
to the end
of my first sentence

now it's the floor
that walks towards me
on unnamed bones
the calcium ground
into flour to rise in bread
baked in the metal scale model
of an apostle's lung

i denounce hunger to feed light

replace the fluid in the veins
with no fluid in the veins
to think absence into solid form
perhaps a cube
that yesterday was sand
and today is covered in bark
waiting to shed itself
somewhere in an autoqueue of insects
patrolling the smallest stains
left by a wounded nightmare
that has every chance
but no hope
of waking up

the fool climbs the mountain
to view what wise men forget →
paints a landscape in intricate detail
with a brush crafted from hair
from his own eyebrows
when complete
paints over it entire in white
only to paint over it again in black
then return with his picture
to sell it to his shadow
at a cold price determined
by the accuracy of memory

as a target
i make love
to the vantage point
of the arrow
not the arrow itself (→)
blind enough
to smell the space

buffering a plain cross
on a forehead light years away
as close as the fingertips
of the archer's cocked hand

no doubt
this is someone ←
who ably presents himself
at the unmanned counter
in this library of violence
who seeks to withdraw
the necessity of the act
but not the act itself
ably inscribed
with the same nail
as a fate of individual numbers
prominent on leathered organs
captive in vinegar
in jars that do not end a line
which one day will tilt
and draw itself back
towards the eye
as it ignites a vigil of burning tongues
that give off words instead of smoke
either side of the second sky
traded entire for the first seed
planted dark into new silence

(o)

i am the animals limping to the blood dairy

i am the gold i inject into every iris

i am the key inserted in the earth

↕

you carve the night
into a somersault
and pray you end up
under its feet

u.

your new design for the sun has one flaw.

the spoon

the spoon with which you eat off yourself

powdered diamonds in a paste
piped from ankle to thigh
in a Cape to Cairo line
that tells us that all Rhodes
lead to here ←

tadpole apostrophes
navigate conjunctive saliva-lust
from the tongue as wave machine

changing mosaics
on the roof of the mouth
feel the jaw move like a bulldozer
about to rubble the one room
in the house reserved for speech

grout from tile and teeth
elocute clouds in the gum-pink
of particle rhetoric

snuff deep in airways
drilled through the spiritual autism
of dissolving space

black candles are placed
not just in the eye sockets
but in the sockets of sleep itself

wax pools as two oceans in miniature
to trap what was seen

before it was there

the inherited ratio
of what is not believed
to what is thought to be true
straightens the ribs to surveyor pegs
to stake out the new estate
on your skin

wooden bones
alight under a halfmoon
force those with the power to decide
to notice your shipwrecked anatomy

your emigrant fingerprints
picked from leaf litter
by a butcher bird

the prodigal departure
of all senses
to nowhere

i have remembered silence
in its own words

taught the train
to stop over my chest
so i can get on

inside the carriage
you are sat at a balsa table
the length of another's life

& in the next carriage
in your livestream audition
as a TV chef you demonstrate

how to simmer an eyeball in your hand
↕   ↕
how to coach fibre-rich words
from your mouth to the plate

cut to the last carriage
where the act of saying grace
is being injected into your lips
as a cosmetic prayer

one object
registered as missing
in a metallurgist's mind
alleges hypnotism in a brunette lasso

the spoon with which you eat yourself

there is no way to repair shadows while we're alive

i heat the stone until its eye opens

invite its callus-scraped duct
to extrude lava in sentences

memory magma
pushes through an axial sleeve
from a thousand miles down
to pull unsigned clouds
out of our subdivided sky

our heads change shape
according to their reminiscence
rally in coherent protest
against themselves

as objects
we are anaesthetised surfaces
our skin wrapping paper for gravity
gifted to any clock that would open its mouth
on its birthday

this is because ←

a falling question
has the same value
as a standing prayer

to misunderstand
is to believe why
you're here

these corners will be constructed
at the same rate at which
they are demolished

here is the box they had made for our eyelids   ←

the mirrors we put in the oven are burning   ←

the bone density of fate is not a test you pass   ←

our mutual appetites for sleep & certainty
require that we wear rope pyjamas

as two notes
we hang unplayed
on a guitarist's hand

our perfume in his fingerprint
is discussed like wine

as the nurse who saves us
becomes our wound so our writing
can remove the bandages
from these words

to decide how the eye
is decided in its illusion
in its sublimated history
squeezed from the backbone
of the last known comma
to pappus-fall and settle
in the impossible molasses
inside the blind nib
of a black cone

to believe
is to misunderstand why
you're here

→

→

→

their wooden lips undress
splinters in our blood

having been removed
i necessarily remain
where i am

to brush full stops
from your jugular notch
with a blue feather

to follow the room through its door

although this echo ←
was caught murdering our sound
they still lowered our bodies
into each other's ears
until we could not hear
what we were saying →

now they expect us
to remove the skin
from the candle

in wax resist our portraits sting
as much as the incor/rectly dial/led
phone number of a hornet

in uncurtained red
our emergencies always seem closer
than they really are

now they expect us
to have our corneas stacked
at either end of this sentence
to calmly patent our veins
as a new form of writing
that can safely diffuse blood
through ag-pipe pores
under a dead language

even without hands
the onus is on us
to reshuffle glass cards

(⇄)

every day
you stand under the question mark
you had made into a shower head
& present yourself with an award
for becoming the drain

there are only five minutes in a lifetime
when you can sell your head back to the womb
to make yourself a prophet

as it turns out
you will not be given permission
to replant memories into your eyeball

you can however
use your eyelashes as a rake
to till the mirror

this is the line in which you will dredge for silence ←

(   )

the exit sign is breathing →

the necessity of waiting until you're gone before you speak to yourself

we pull the philosopher's body
out of a sinkhole
in her own chest

mank hair
pauses a psalm
over her face

cochineal bruise on her breast
an inauthentic stigmata
lodging complaints beneath her skin
as we splint the bamboo in her arms
lift her up not holding her down
in her sudden role as collapsed christ

in this moment ←
we dangle her toes
in the figure eight sweep
of a hog hair brush
in a newly opened tin
of black paint

we stretch the skin from her hands
tight over the lamp in the lighthouse
to project her fingerprints onto the horizon

this coal fired transience
permits our future to exist
where we began

she had said there is no such thing

as open ocean in a closed world
because we cannot see how history
squeezes the planet like a soft toy
& every full stop ever printed
is in fact a linguatomic moon
whose orbit delineates our predicted
absence

apostrophes
also presume to float (   )
as they mark out comas
in your own history

you are the nail
hammered direct
into the grammar
of suggestion

this is the light
before light existed

a gleaming hound's tooth
dressed red in your vein
precisely one hour before
it blocks the passage to the heart

precisely one hour before
the legs on the chair
become snakes to milk in
the ground around you
with unchided venom

you are shown
the electrolysis in your brain
in its display case

you never imagined
you could sleep
without witnesses

as you sleep
you rehearse the birth
of your final child

the heads drawing blood
from their heads are
drawing heads with the
blood from their heads

you pack your head
in its suitcase three times
to find it still on the bed
grinning like the unbreakable
mirror it is convinced
it can re-gift itself
to an earthquake undecided
what scale it should use
when reducing two continents
to one alleviated thought →

there is a hearse
at the traffic lights
that will never turn green

you walk the house
with stones between your toes
as a way of incubating
the next ice age
in your memory

a ladder cannot be convinced
to climb down from itself

. i watch him knit a mirror with his eyes

watch him cast the first stone into original memory
to see it skim towards the same mirror
now propped up against the horizon
shattered like glass fingernails from a wailing wall
as we ourselves alternate as gold teeth
exploding inside this mica mouth
spines smelted into the slightest answers
inside our own ears floating in open ocean
as wishing wells for the drowned
as deep as any word our heads pop up
to compete for the dot on the i in genesis

your licence to create the opening dream sequence has been revoked

enclosed are the instructions
on how to design a life
while walking the dog
so it can sniff out the bones
in your own grave

)…strike gently away from body…(

in a downbeat of the psyche
your necklace lets go
scattering toes & fingers
in Bren gun slow audio
across the heirloom oak table
in another Pacific War drama
shot through a Vaseline lens

)...strike gently away from body...(

you stop in at the dry cleaner
to collect your skin only to be told
that the stains cannot be removed
without extra cost and that the only currency
accepted in this establishment is the soul

)...strike gently away from body...(

this list is predetermined:

      1 stand here while your tongue is dissolved in wine
      2 spend more time teaching dust to speak
      3 permit yourself to learn the botanical names of lies

without regret
i fall into my father's mouth
sucked back through his cigar butt
spat onto his bullock's eye

asleep
his eyelids become trampolines
rebounding one eternal seed
between here & hereafter
blindsided he sees everything
in his wake

the soft grenade in his hand
contains no messages for the future

i watch him separate each lip of its colour
before these words form

)...strike gently away from body...(

orbiting shadows
intervene with grace
in a burning wheelchair

to let down what we couldn't lift
to let down what we couldn't lift

you catch yourself wading
through your own ability
to scold the light

you take aim
at the world
with one thought
& realise you are
the target ←

you catch yourself wading
through your own ability
to scold the light
for being silent

)...strike gently away from body...(

how to replace the washer
to stop blood leeching into the cloud
above your head

do you remember
how we would hover
above each other in sleep

how we perfected the art
of waking up in the wrong body
at the right time

in our blinking
our jellyfish propulsion
through evolution

i was the first person in history to close a door .

selling meaning in negative space

for Gordon

this thought is a challenge to what this thought is

this statement was on the point of collapse when your reading commenced

this line is the lost opportunity you never had

a careful reading of the self
offers a menu of glowing dust
on a mirror   (46-)

he is wearing full body armour
made from fingernails from those he saved

& their fingernails are still growing   (19-)

he never talks without being asleep in his own words

he talks miracles down from their own end

in defence of the head i cut it off

nowadays they just eat the heads cold   (34-)

i am not all the reasons i am

i sing to myself in the wrong room til i'm dead

i burn safely til i'm lit (25-)

what you can't see behind this page

is the same dog is the same dog
barking rhetoric through your head   (20-)

there are no ghosts in this exhibition

these prayers are not satisfied with this life

ghosts are not in these walls ghosts are these walls
ghosts are not on these walls ghosts are these walls
only ghosts are exhibited

> only walls
> can be seen
> where ghosts were
> not held
> against their will
> was also their way
> out   (57-)

every breath the punch-line in this long running joke against definition

if nothing else these words provide instruction on how to trip silence   (23-)

trip the silence trip
the silence trip the
silence TRIP the silence
trip the silence trip
the silence TRIP the
silence trip the silence
trip the silence TRIP (28-)

> punished to a solitary breath
> every thing forgiven is given to him
> in a bag of air imprisoned

for just such an occasion
the occasion is just
what is called a life not yet pumped
from the scrotum of a male clock (42-)

inexplicably the sake in for the sake of has been reached

when i'm this tired i can only be asleep inside my own erection (24-)

hot & cold taps
supplant eye sockets
in a skull
to drip
the absolute
through a hole
in his hand (20-)

in less functional circumstance a scream could   be inserted here

this is what happens when premonition loses   its keys

the spare key is under   the mat but the mat   is on fire

as only a notion can
it tramples the marigolds
in the front garden
visors its hands over its face
to squint through its sole window
to see buckets of tears
being thrown over tomorrow's sunset (67-)

the primary witness to all this   was standing here

the witness fled   as your reading approached

the vacancy created   can now be filled with something else

perhaps   an open ended aphorism which could be true but isn't

a short notice at short notice

DENIAL IS THE SUREST PATH TO ADMISSION   (50-)

in continuing to read these words
you are their primary source of damage

you have just rewritten them all in all possible ways

you have just reread your own absence   (30-)

another deaf cloud said what before i could say nothing

another fashion for mixing concrete with the tongue

another way of turning leaves into platelets for the blood   (28-)

don't listen don't listen don't
listen don't listen don't listen
don't listen don't listen don't
escape   (16-)

to determine the weight of the stone

                    observe the size of the hand
                    about to throw it   (17-)

        what was held in this sentence is now lost to you

                    it's about now
                    that we get to see
                    the hero
                    accuse his own skin
                    of lying   (27-)

                            at night
                            anchors are thrown out
                            from the corners of his eyes
                            to moor his head to its pillow   (19-)

        simply writing the word lost does not guarantee i won't be found in this sentence

                            i was given a carry bag for the hemispheres   (24-)

                                    he throws the dice
                                    knowing the dice
                                    will never land   (10-)

        this blue square
        has been placed here
        as a device to distract
        the flow of your reading

        this is not a blue square   (23-)

my feet ask more questions of me than i do

even drowned you can still strain yourself out of the water

to the left of the left margin
you will see the bodies
at the base of the cliff (18-)

                              to the right of the right margin
                              you will see the queue
                              beginning its ascent (15-)

a lull in proceedings has been identified

    it is suggested that you continue to dig up these words with this shovel

        while i pan for the full stop made of gold (31-)

                              he can only fall
                              if the earth is put back
                              beneath his feet (13-)

the seven wounded heads of memory
each the shape of the thing forgotten

        or did i say

        each shape the thing forgotten

a memory had is had had no memory had is had no where is had had no thing

or to recall or

the fainter if the fainter the recall the stronger the glue for the door

if you show me the door
i'll show you how all three of us were found
holding hands in this grave (79-)

he attends the funeral of text but is not there

death forged this signature to tell itself apart (18-)

CONGRATULATIONS

you are now standing in the room
where souls are marked with a felt-tip pen for surgery

you will be asked to undress until
your bones are suffused with enough lead to
enable you to fall painlessly through
the unushering floor of this paginate hotel

when no one is left every one is there (55-)

HOWEVER

not finding enough animals
to drink enough blood
aspurt via his index fingers
his conscience swells

                                        to the size of a small planet   (24-)

i collect his sweat in a teaspoon
from the bottom corner of a mirror
under the threat of invasion   (19-)

                        veins were the first thread

                        shadows the first cloth   (9-)

if you do not answer this question i'll know you are here   (12-)

        the red square is
        another less surprising attempt
        to squarumvent your eyes
        by making them bypass
        more purposeful markings
        that would seek to form
        your overall reading

        this square is red   (32-)

            yes these rayon folds are inside the only eye i claim to recognise

        yes as large as it is i will carry this pandanus tree to the underworld   (28-)

while cutting the toenails of the hero
my own toenails grow straight into the ground   (15-)

                        he is tying knots in the throats of arrows
                        until the targets confess   (13-)

to replicate the head
into enough arrows
to allow St Sebastian
to grin sustenance
into a well targeted meal
without cold confession   (22-)

he has been arrested by light
his body is being turned away
for all & no one to see
his wrists cuffed with the infinite (25-)

you have walked this far with candles between your toes

if you kneel your legs will explode (17-)

every button
has just been ripped off
every shirt in the world
by the realisation
that every shirt is a spy
correcting the grammar
in every torso
but one (29-)

when i am again one atom
he will again be the one
to split me as a private sun
unskilled in every blindness (23-)

the reader has been defined the reader has been defined do not define the reader
the reader has been defined the reader has been defined do not define the (29-)

on even numbered days of the week you are asked to use ending one

ending one

      braiding live earthworms into a loam–hungry sheet
      he lies down to wait for no one to wait for him (35-)

        on odd numbered days of the week you are asked to use ending two

   ending two

          braiding live earthworms into a loam–hungry sheet
          he lies down to wait for one no to wait for him   (35-)

----

total occupation (bruised)   = **1266-**
total occupation (unbruised) = zero

Notes

'epigraph': From the poem *Fratello Campana* (Bell Brother) by Assunta Strada; (*Quarantaquattro Scalini*—Badia a Elmi Editore, 2016). Translation Simone Gelli.

'mixed memory on paper': The stanzas commencing 'in complete privacy' and 'nothing is more alien' use manipulated fragments from a 1958 interview with Giorgio Morandi by Édouard Roditi. The stanza 'he had stopped working' uses a quote from a notated drawing of Morandi by Brett Whiteley. Whiteley visited Morandi in 1960, noting that Morandi was upset because his favourite pear tree had been cut down.

'from the other side of the shark': Small sections and phrases are taken from *Fishes of Australia*, E.M. Grant (E.M. Grant Pty Ltd, Scarborough, 1987) and *Guide to Fishes*, E.M. Grant (Department of Harbours and Marine, Brisbane, 1982). Vic Hislop is a shark hunter from Queensland who sold Damien Hirst the tiger shark the artist used in his work *The Physical Impossibility of Death in the Mind of Someone Living*.

See also the corresponding sequence *Angstcination* by B.R. Dionysius in *Plumwood Mountain* (2015).

'silent approach': c. 1924. oil on board by Clarice Beckett, collection NGA. After her death, her former teacher Max Meldrum graded her work based on how closely Beckett had applied the tenets of his theory of Australian Tonalism.

'the stained glass windows of the world are coming': Commission piece for *Moving Words* (QAGOMA 2018), curated by Queensland Poetry Festival. Sections of this work use quotations by D Harding either literally or in a treated format. Sources for those words are the publication *Body of Objects* (IMA); the program *Colour Theory* (NITV); and an interview on GOMA TV. The poem title is from a conversation with D at Milani Gallery in October 2017. *Wall Composition in Reckitt's Blue* was a site-specific work in GOMA. The poem draws on a number of Harding's works.

The black squares throughout the poem are an in-scale design (1:82) for a multipurpose silicone cube.

'portable eyes remit subconscious colour in black': Small areas of text in the 'comma' & 'circle' sections include improvised fragments sourced from the James Gleeson Oral History Collection (NGA) in his interview with Alun Leach-Jones. *gray via its american spelling* refers to the poet Robert Gray. The circle-in-square symbol used throughout the poem is a simple allusion to Alun's *Noumenon* series.

'[stillife]': This suite is based on specific B&W photographs by Neil Griffith from his *dead life* series.

'the black hand of Badia Elmi'. Italic sections in this poem are from the following sources:
you might say to these mulberry trees…—paraphrase of Luke 17:6. *in such momentous circumstance alone*—Dante, *The Divine Comedy*—Purgatory—Canto 33 (trans. Henry F. Cary). *where all the water runs backwards*—Boccaccio, *The Decameron*—Sixth Day—Tale 10 (trans. Richard Aldington). *i did not change my mind…*—paraphrase of Boccaccio, *The Decameron*—Tenth Day—Tale 3 (trans. Richard Aldington). *as entire and sound as it ever was*—Boccaccio, *The Decameron*—Sixth Day—Tale 10 (trans. Richard Aldington).

'the water carries me to myself': Commission piece for the exhibition and publication *My River* (2013) at the Counihan Gallery In Brunswick, (Moreland City Council).

'rain as narrative': Edda Dell'Orso is a singer well known for her wordless vocals in many Italian film scores. The line 'the face of the waters' is from Genesis 1:2.

'the naked driver': Commission piece for the exhibition *David Malouf and Friends*, Museum of Brisbane 2014. The line *this tender conceptual blue* is taken from David Malouf's poem *Moonflower* (*Typewriter Music*, UQP 2007).

'… learning to cry without eyes': Commission piece for *Brisbane Poetry Map* organised by the Queensland Poetry Festival—sponsored by CAL and Brisbane City Council. Michael Parekōwhai's sculpture *The World Turns* (GOMA) is situated at Kurilpa Point. The end of the poem alludes the murder of French student Sophie Collombet whose body was found nearby.

'twofold': Based on the painting *Evening, Canaipa* (1998) by Gordon Shepherdson.

'the skin is sent to name the body': Based on the sculpture *St Bartholomew Flayed* (1562) by Marco d'Agrate in Milan Cathedral. Some scholars believe that St Bartholomew and Nathanael of Cana are the same person.

'selling meaning in negative space': The text has been reconfigured in small ways to adjust the poem to the scale of this book. In its original publication the numbers throughout the poem are printed in red. (see *Prizing Diversity*, Thames and Hudson, 2015).

Acknowledgements

Works in this collection were written on Turrbul, Jagera and Gubbi Gubbi land. I acknowledge the traditional custodians and pay my respects to Elders past, present and emerging.

Thank you to Shane Strange and the editorial board at Recent Work Press for permitting this book to surface. Thank you to family Eve Fraser, Ariel Shepherdson, Isaak Shepherdson, Luke Shepherdson, and to poets/travellers Elisa Biagini, Pascalle Burton, Margie Cronin, Matt Hetherington, Anna Jacobson, Max Mandorlo, Felicity Plunkett, David Stavanger, Melinda Smith, and Tom Shapcott for their continuing conversations, insights, and support. Thank you to Neil Griffith for photographing the cover image. Thank you to ghosts known and unknown for keeping my address on file for the beautifully packaged silences.

Some works in this collection were previously published in *Cordite, Shearsman* (UK), *Verity La, StylusLit, Dispatches from the Poetry Wars* (US), *Prizing Diversity* (The Josephine Ulrick Prizes 1998—2014), *David Malouf and Friends* (MoB), *Australian Book Review—States of Poetry Queensland—Series One, signs* (University of Canberra Vice-Chancellor's International Poetry Prize 2018), *UNDERNEATH* (University of Canberra Vice-Chancellor's International Poetry Prize 2015), *Arc Poetry* (CAN), *Voyages* (IT), *Meanjin.*

www.ingramcontent.com/pod-product-compliance
Ingram Content Group Australia Pty Ltd
76 Discovery Rd, Dandenong South VIC 3175, AU
AUHW020639050325
407891AU00002B/18

9 780645 651218